I0809781

ARENA EVENTS

MUSIC CONCERTS

KENNY ABDO

Fly!
An Imprint of Abdo Zoom
abdobooks.com

abdobooks.com

Published by Abdo Zoom, a division of ABDO, P.O. Box 398166, Minneapolis, Minnesota 55439. Copyright © 2019 by Abdo Consulting Group, Inc. International copyrights reserved in all countries. No part of this book may be reproduced in any form without written permission from the publisher. Fly!™ is a trademark and logo of Abdo Zoom.

Printed in the United States of America, North Mankato, Minnesota.
092018
012019

THIS BOOK CONTAINS RECYCLED MATERIALS

Photo Credits: Alamy, Getty Images, Shutterstock, ©Cangminzho p10/CC BY-SA 4.0
Production Contributors: Kenny Abdo, Jennie Forsberg, Grace Hansen
Design Contributors: Dorothy Toth, Neil Klinepier

Library of Congress Control Number: 2018946199

Publisher's Cataloging-in-Publication Data

Names: Abdo, Kenny, author.
Title: Music concerts / by Kenny Abdo.
Description: Minneapolis, Minnesota : Abdo Zoom, 2019 | Series: Arena events | Includes online resources and index.
Identifiers: ISBN 9781532125362 (lib. bdg.) | ISBN 9781641856812 (pbk) | ISBN 9781532126383 (ebook) | ISBN 9781532126895 (Read-to-me ebook)
Subjects: LCSH: Concerts--Juvenile literature. | Music--Performance--Juvenile literature. | Music festivals--Juvenile literature.
Classification: DDC 781.6607--dc23

TABLE OF CONTENTS

MUSIC CONCERTS

Rocking out in the arenas of the world, music concerts have gotten people to sing and dance for generations!

FESTIVAL
GUIDE

Music has been called "the medicine of the mind." Studies have shown that going to concerts can reduce stress and improve your mood greatly.

OPENING ACT

Historians have found that musical **traditions** helped early humans **communicate** and form tighter social **bonds**.

Music has been played as far back as the **Ice Age**. A flute made out of vulture bone 40,000 years ago was recently discovered in southern Germany.

The first known public concert that charged a **cover** was held in London in 1672. Violinist John Banister played for an audience at his home in Whitefriars.

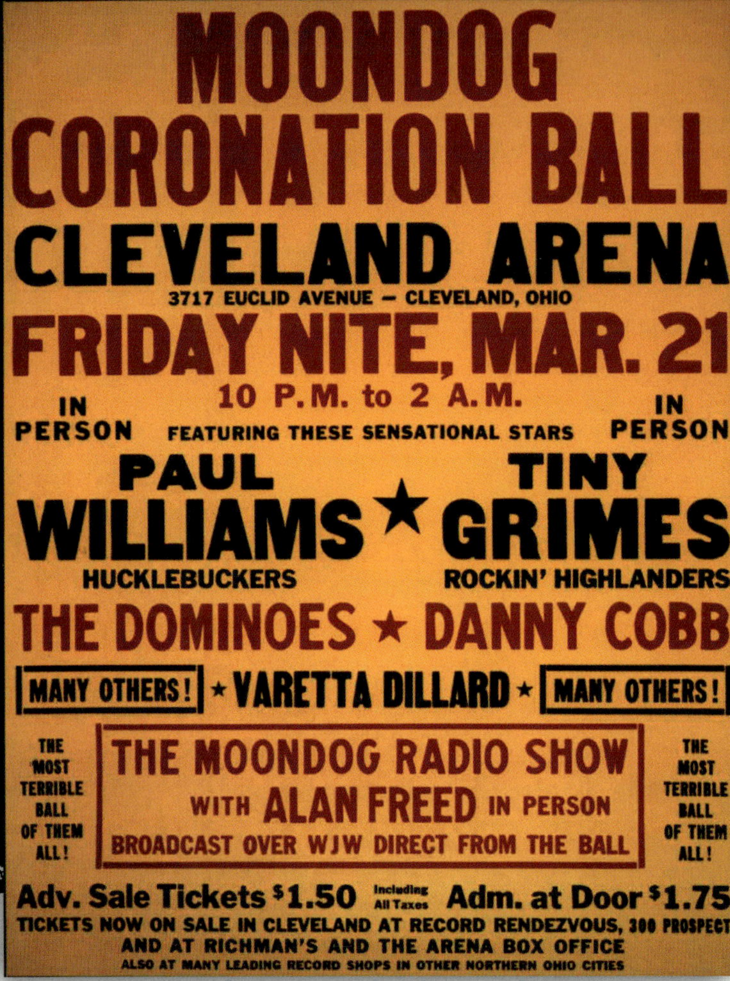

The Moondog Coronation Ball is considered to be the first major rock concert in history. It was in Cleveland, Ohio, on March 21, 1952. The arena could only hold 10,000 people. More than 25,000 showed up to party.

THE MAIN EVENT

In 2017, more than 68 million concert tickets were sold in North America. That is more than 8 billion dollars in ticket sales!

The Philippine Arena in Bulacan is the largest indoor arena in the world. It can hold up to 55,000 people. Katy Perry was the first **international** solo artist to hold a concert there in 2015.

Metallica is the only band in history to have played concerts on all seven **continents**. They broke this record after performing in Antarctica in 2013.

GLOSSARY

bond – a feeling or shared interest that brings people together.

communicate – to share knowledge, thoughts, or feelings.

continent – one of Earth's seven main land areas.

cover – a fee paid for access into a concert.

Ice Age – a period of time between 1.8 million years ago and 11,500 years ago that includes several ice ages. An ice age is a time when thick ice sheets cover large areas of land.

international – of or relating to more than one nation.

tradition – a belief, a custom, or a story handed down from older people to younger people.

ONLINE RESOURCES

Booklinks
NONFICTION NETWORK
FREE! ONLINE NONFICTION RESOURCES

To learn more about music concerts, please visit abdobooklinks.com. These links are routinely monitored and updated to provide the most current information available.

INDEX